BRITAIN BY NIGHT

MARK McNEILL

AMBERLEY

First published 2022

Amberley Publishing
The Hill, Stroud
Gloucestershire, GL5 4EP

www.amberley-books.com

Copyright © Mark McNeill, 2022

The right of Mark McNeill to be identified as the Author of this work has been
asserted in accordance with the Copyrights, Designs and Patents Act 1988.

ISBN 978 1 3981 0245 3 (print)
ISBN 978 1 3981 0246 0 (ebook)

British Library Cataloguing in Publication Data.
A catalogue record for this book is available from the British Library.

Typesetting by SJmagic DESIGN SERVICES, India.
Printed in the UK.

ACKNOWLEDGEMENTS

A big thank you to my wife and family – Maisy, Martha and Hope – for putting up with lots of late nights. Thank you to Professor Brian Cox and Tim Peake for giving me support and sharing my photographs on social media. A big thank you to Dave Zdanowicz for all his help and advice on all things book related, and for recommending a few brilliant Yorkshire locations to visit. A massive thanks goes to the makers of the equipment I have used: to Nikon for the camera; Formatt Hitech for their continued support and Nightscape filter, which helps reduce light pollution; 3 Legged Thing for epic, sturdy tripods; and to OPPO UK for their OPPO Find X5 Pro mobile phone, which helped me capture shots in London.

ABOUT THE PHOTOGRAPHER

Mark McNeill, a landscape and astro photographer from the north-west of England, has a passion for landscape photography that started over fifteen years ago. Some of his favourite locations are based in the English Lake District and Glencoe, Scotland. He won the award for Astronomy Photographer of the Year in 2018 with his image *Me Versus the Galaxy*, which was in the People and Space category. It was featured in *National Geographic* magazine and by Collins Astronomy. He has had features in Sigma Lounge, and *Practical Photography* magazine shortlisted him for Science Photographer of the Year in 2021 for the Royal Photographic Society.

Website: markmcneillphotography.com

INTRODUCTION

The idea for this book was to try and capture Britain in a unique way. Most people take photos during the day; well, I get a buzz out of taking photos at night, so I thought I'd travel the whole of Britain.

I journeyed from my home town in Preston to Scotland, Wales, Northumberland, the east coast, London, Manchester, Liverpool, Birmingham – you name it, I tried to travel there. I travelled to lots of places and didn't even manage to take a photo due to rain, wind or traffic. So many things got in my way – even Covid-19.

The images are mainly of famous landmarks in our towns and cities. Some of the most amazing places are in the darker locations, such as Northumberland, the Lake District, Hermitage Castle in the Scottish Borders, and Anglesey in Wales. Even more exciting is the capital city,

London, or the city centre of Manchester – adding the movement of cars and buses adds a bit of interest into a busy area.

I really hope you enjoy these images and that you have a chance to visit some of these places. It might even inspire you to take similar photos near where you live or, perhaps, when it gets dark, to venture a little further out and try and capture some further afield. A good tip, I would say, is always try and bring a tripod with you, or rest your camera on something like a wall or beanbag. When you do night photography you need to do long exposures, mainly because it's so dark, and you need to hold the camera for at least five to ten seconds to capture an image. So, if you're not able to hold it steady the images will turn out blurry. That is my top tip of the day!

Edinburgh

Edinburgh

New Forth crossing, Edinburgh

Kelpies

Kelpies

St Abb's Head Lighthouse

Queensferry

Glasgow Co-operative building

River Clyde, Glasgow

Riverside Museum, Glasgow

Tradeston Bridge, Glasgow

Glasgow

Renfrew

Cottage, Glencoe

Hermitage Castle

Falkirk Wheel

Lindisfarne Castle

Lindisfarne

Lindisfarne Causeway

Bathing house, Craster

Bathing house, Northumberland

Great Stone of Fourstones

Alnwick Castle

Bamburgh Castle

Sycamore Gap

Allonby Beach

Derwent Water

Keswick

Ambleside

Satellites over Kirkstone Pass

Piel Island

Twistleton Scar

Kendal

Castlerigg Stone Circle

Newcastle Castle

Angel of the North

Northern Spire Bridge

Tynemouth Priory and Castle

St Mary's Lighthouse, Whitley

York Minster

York city walls

Harrogate Odeon

Transport Bridge, River Tees

Knaresborough

Haworth

Huddersfield

Whitby Abbey

Leeds

Staithes

Saltburn Pier

Saltaire Mill, Bradford

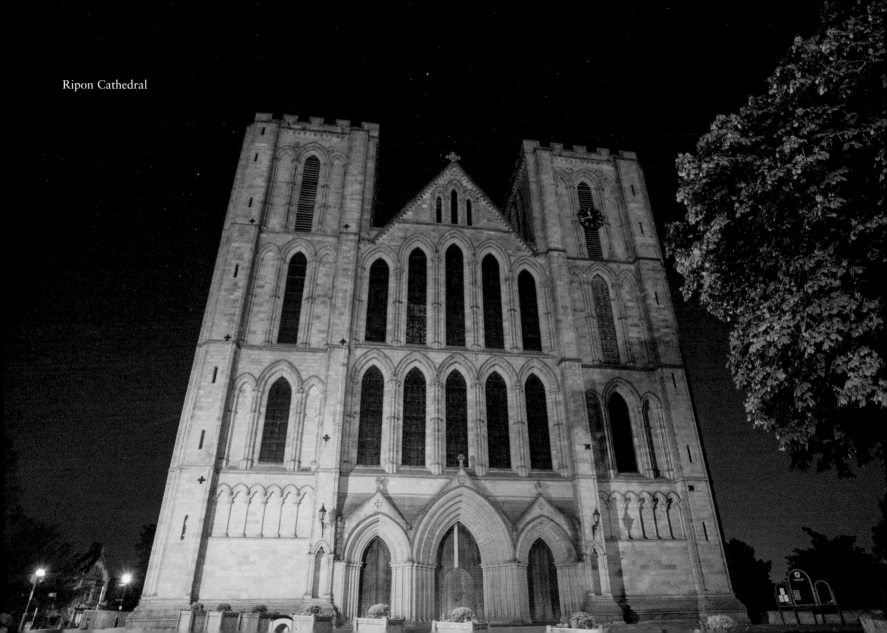

Ripon Cathedral

Darwen Tower

Bolton city centre

Bolton Town
Hall

The Big One

Blackpool

Ashton Memorial

Spitfire Memorial, Fairhaven

W3644

Preston bus station

Lancaster Castle

Hornby Castle

Littledale Free Church

Lytham Windmill

Singing Ringing Tree, Burnley

St Anne's Beach

Marshaw Wyre, Forest of Bowland

Manchester Arndale

Manchester

Manchester

Trinity Way, Manchester

Piccadilly views, Manchester

Stockport Plaza

River Irwell, Salford

Salford Quays

Salford Quays

Birkenhead to Liverpool

Liverpool city centre

Jodrell Bank, Cheshire

Silver Jubilee Bridge, Runcorn

Chester

Buxton

Magpie Mine

Magpie Mine

Chapel-en-le-Frith

Winnats Pass

'Crooked Spire', Chesterfield

Dukes Drive Viaduct, Buxton

Old Market Square, Nottingham

Nottingham city centre

Newark Castle

Lincoln

Boston Stump

Ironbridge

Wolverhampton

South Stacks

Cardiff

Cardiff

Wales Millennium Centre, Cardiff

Menai Bridge

Caernarfon Castle

'Church in the Sea', Anglesey

Birmingham

Birmingham

Gas Street Basin, Birmingham

Chamberlain Square, Birmingham

Radcliffe Camera, Oxford

St Albans

Star trails over the *Cutty Sark*

Big Ben

The London Eye

Clifton Suspension Bridge, Bristol

Gold Hill, Shaftesbury